*To snow lovers everywhere —B.R.*

*For Finn, Scarlett, Madeleine, and Dan,*
*who all love to spend time in the snow —B.C.*

Thanks to math consultant Pondie Taylor, Interventionist at St. Paul City School in
St. Paul, MN, for reviewing the text.

Millbrook Press™
An imprint of Lerner Publishing Group, Inc.
241 First Avenue North
Minneapolis, MN 55401 USA

For reading levels and more information, look up this title at www.lernerbooks.com.

Designed by Athena Currier.
Main body text set in Bulmer MT Std. Typeface provided by Monotype Typography.
The illustrations for this book were created using a combination of paper collage and digital illustration.
First, the characters and background elements were created by hand by cutting pieces of painted
paper, which were glued in place to give the feeling of dynamic movement. These were then
scanned and placed in the page setting, for which the background was digitally painted. Finally,
the snowflakes were counted and placed on a top layer of the illustration, arranged to depict the
snow movement as described in the text.

**Library of Congress Cataloging-in-Publication Data**

The Cataloging-in-Publication Data for *The Power of Snow* is on file at the Library of Congress.
ISBN 978-1-7284-5091-9 (lib. bdg.)
ISBN 979-8-7656-0208-9 (epub)

Manufactured in the United States of America
1-50590-50056-1/11/2023

# the POWER of SNOW

**BOB RACZKA**

Illustrated by **BRYONY CLARKSON**

Millbrook Press / Minneapolis

Two flakes play.

$2^1 = 2$ to the first power

$2 = 2$

Four flakes sashay.

$2^2$ = 2 to the second power

$2 \times 2 = 4$

Eight flakes twirl.

$2^3 = 2$ to the third power

$2 \times 2 \times 2 = 8$

Sixteen flakes swirl.

$2^4$ = 2 to the fourth power

$2 \times 2 \times 2 \times 2 = 16$

Thirty-two flakes flurry.

$2^5 =$ 2 to the fifth power

$2 \times 2 \times 2 \times 2 \times 2 = 32$

Sixty-four flakes scurry.

$2^6$ = 2 to the sixth power

$2 \times 2 \times 2 \times 2 \times 2 \times 2 = 64$

One hundred twenty-eight flakes drift.

$2^7 = $ 2 to the seventh power

$2 \times 2 \times 2 \times 2 \times 2 \times 2 \times 2 = 128$

Two hundred fifty-six flakes sift.

$2^8 =$ 2 to the eighth power

$2 \times 2 \times 2 \times 2 \times 2 \times 2 \times 2 \times 2 = 256$

Five hundred twelve flakes whoosh.

$2^9$ = 2 to the ninth power

$2 \times 2 \times 2 \times 2 \times 2 \times 2 \times 2 \times 2 \times 2 = 512$

One thousand twenty-four flakes swoosh.

$2^{10}$ = 2 to the tenth power

$2 \times 2 \times 2 \times 2 \times 2 \times 2 \times 2 \times 2 \times 2 \times 2 = 1{,}024$

Two thousand forty-eight flakes cluster.

$2^{11}$ = 2 to the eleventh power

$2 \times 2 \times 2 \times 2 \times 2 \times 2 \times 2 \times 2 \times 2 \times 2 \times 2 = 2{,}048$

Four thousand ninety-six flakes bluster.

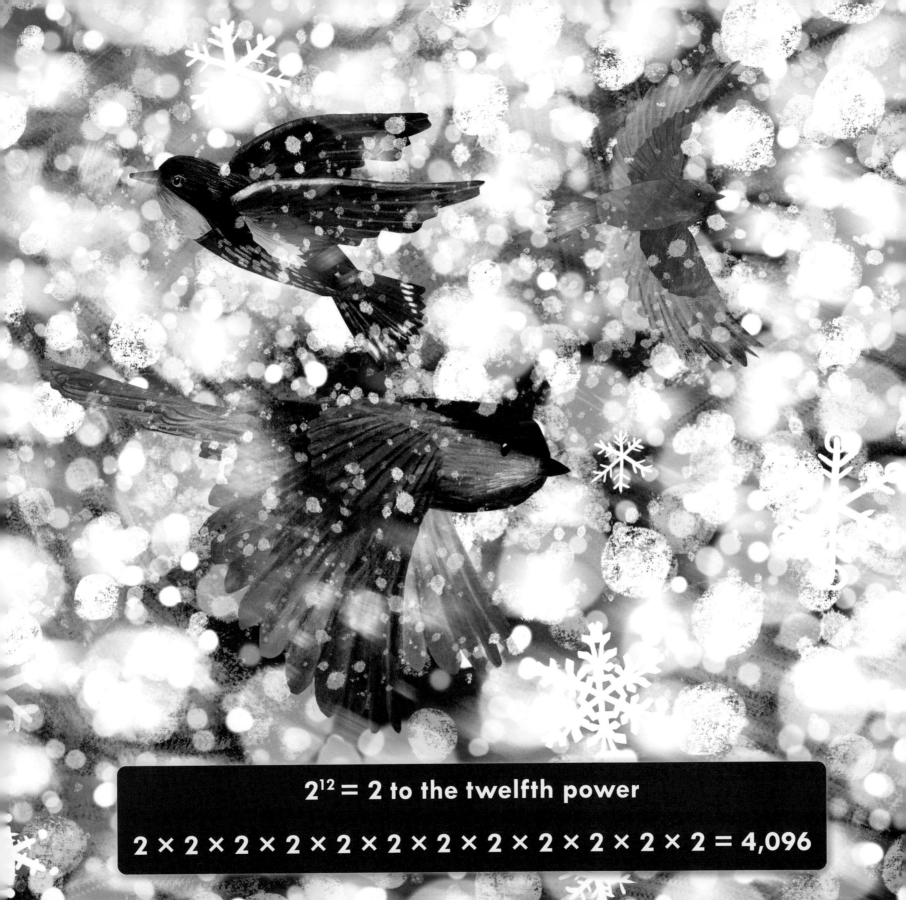

$2^{12}$ = 2 to the twelfth power

$2 \times 2 \times 2 \times 2 \times 2 \times 2 \times 2 \times 2 \times 2 \times 2 \times 2 \times 2 = 4{,}096$

Eight thousand one hundred ninety-two flakes swarm.

$$2^{13} = 2 \text{ to the thirteenth power}$$

$$2 \times 2 \times 2 \times 2 \times 2 \times 2 \times 2 \times 2 \times 2 \times 2 \times 2 \times 2 \times 2 = 8{,}192$$

Sixteen thousand three hundred eighty-four flakes storm.

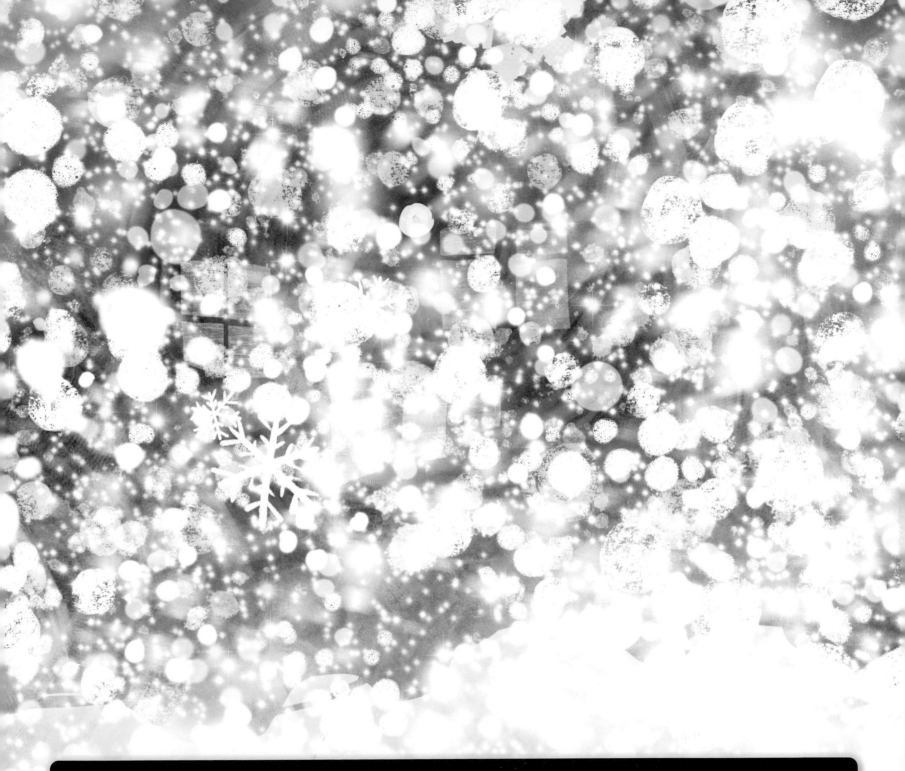

$$2^{14} = 2 \text{ to the fourteenth power}$$

$$2 \times 2 \times 2 \times 2 \times 2 \times 2 \times 2 \times 2 \times 2 \times 2 \times 2 \times 2 \times 2 \times 2 = 16{,}384$$

One snow day.

Two friends play.

$$2^1 = 2 \text{ to the first power}$$

$$2 = 2$$

# What Is an Exponent?

*The Power of Snow* demonstrates the power of special numbers called exponents. We use exponents as a simpler way to show a number being multiplied over and over again. Think of exponents as a shortcut for writing longer math problems.

What does an exponent look like? It's a small number that appears immediately after a regular number and slightly higher, like the $4$ in $2^4$.

We read $2^4$ as "two to the fourth power." The number 2 is called the base. The base tells us what number is being multiplied. The smaller number $4$ is called the exponent. The exponent tells us how many times the base is being multiplied. For example:

**$2^4$ means the number 2 multiplied four times: $2 \times 2 \times 2 \times 2$;**

**$3^5$ means the number 3 multiplied five times: $3 \times 3 \times 3 \times 3 \times 3$; and**

**$5^2$ means the number 5 multiplied two times: $5 \times 5$.**

Often the exponents $2$ and $3$ are read another way. $2^2$ may be read as "two squared," and $2^3$ can be read as "two cubed."

As you can see, an exponent is simply a number that tells us how many times to multiply another number. This is especially helpful when the exponent is a higher number. Instead of writing out $2 \times 2 \times 2 \times 2 \times 2 \times 2 \times 2 \times 2 \times 2 \times 2$, we can write $2^{10}$ and read it as "two to the tenth power."

To remember how to read exponents, think of how they have the power to make numbers bigger. The higher the exponent is, the more times the base is multiplied. And the more times the base is multiplied, the bigger the product becomes. For example:

**$2^2$ (two to the second power) means $2 \times 2$, which equals 4;**      **→ $2^2 = 4$**

**$2^3$ (two to the third power) means $2 \times 2 \times 2$, which equals 8; and**    **→ $2^3 = 8$**

**$2^4$ (two to the fourth power) means $2 \times 2 \times 2 \times 2$, which equals 16.**   **→ $2^4 = 16$**

The only exception is when the base is 1. No matter how many times you multiply 1 by itself, the product remains 1.

Did you notice that each time the exponent increases by one, the value gets much bigger?

When the base is 2, the product doubles each time the exponent grows by one (8 is twice as big as 4, and 16 is twice as big as 8). This is called exponential growth.

Exponential growth isn't just a math concept. It happens in real life! A growing baby is one example. It starts out as a single cell that divides into two. Each of those two cells then divides to make four. Then those four cells each divide to make eight. After about nine months of cells dividing, a baby is born. And when that baby grows into an adult, it will have roughly thirty-seven trillion (37,000,000,000,000) cells!

*The Power of Snow* begins with just two snowflakes. But each time you turn the page, the exponent increases by one. And each time the exponent increases by one, the number of snowflakes doubles. That's why, after turning the page just thirteen times, we end up with 16,384 snowflakes!

Here's a quick quiz: if you could turn the page one more time, increasing the exponent by one to show $2^{15}$ snowflakes, how many snowflakes would you see?

# Illustrator's Note

Creating the art for *The Power of Snow* presented one tricky problem: how to show the correct number of snowflakes on each page. For this book, it was important to get the math right! Of course, the first few pages were easy. But as the quantity of flakes increased, it became much harder to count them all. So I worked out a plan. The images were created using different layers, kind of like clear sheets with different parts of the art on each one. I created a certain number of flakes on one layer. Then I duplicated this layer, flipping, scaling, and rotating it to give a natural look. Duplicating the layer allowed me to multiply the exact number of flakes as I worked. I could then add the more detailed snowflakes, counting these out individually to get to the total number. As with real snow, once the flakes became tiny and overlaid, some appear to blend together—but they are all there!

How many are you able to count? Good luck!